Samuel Arthur Bent

Hints on Language in Connection

With sight-reading and writing in primary and intermedfiate schools

Samuel Arthur Bent

Hints on Language in Connection
With sight-reading and writing in primary and intermedfiate schools

ISBN/EAN: 9783337085322

Printed in Europe, USA, Canada, Australia, Japan

Cover: Foto ©Paul-Georg Meister /pixelio.de

More available books at **www.hansebooks.com**

Hints on Language

IN CONNECTION WITH

SIGHT-READING AND WRITING

IN

PRIMARY AND INTERMEDIATE
SCHOOLS

BY

S. ARTHUR BENT, A.M.
SUPERINTENDENT OF THE PUBLIC SCHOOLS OF CLINTON, MASS.

BOSTON
LEE AND SHEPARD PUBLISHERS.
NEW YORK CHARLES T. DILLINGHAM
1886

ELECTROTYPED BY
C. J. PETERS AND SON, BOSTON.

PREFACE.

LANGUAGE-EXERCISE is now found on the programme of most Primary Schools, from the lowest grade upwards. The absence of a text-book, however, on a subject which must be taught orally, makes instruction unsystematic and often unsuccessful. In order to suggest a method of graded class-work, which shall include under the head of Language whatever is taught in reading, writing, form, color, and number, the author offers the following Hints to the profession, on the basis of experiments already attempted by teachers whose assistance is gratefully acknowledged.

S. A. B.

CLINTON, MASS., October, 1885.

CONTENTS.

Grade I.

	PAGE
Language-Teaching. — Its true place	7
Talking as Language	9
Object Lessons in Language	10
The Development Method	11
I See, O See, Developed	12
A Cat, Developed	13
Ran, Developed	15
Review	16
Third Month	17
Writing	18
Sight-Reading	19
Phonic Exercise	22
Thŭgh-book. Ugh-cat	22
Language-Exercises	23
The Cat as Object-Lesson	28
Vocabulary of Three Hundred Words	30

Grade II.

Sight-Reading	33
Definition	37
Spelling	37
Language	38
Picture Lessons	39
Letter-Writing	43

Correct Speech 44
Dictation 45
Number 45
Abstract and Concrete 46

Grade III.

Ink 47
Reading and Number 48
Language 49
Monday's Exercise 49
Tuesday's " 51
Wednesday's " 52
Thursday's " 53
Friday's " 54
Picture-Exercise on the Lion 56
Picture-Exercise on Silk 56
Geography 57
Declamation 58

Grade IV. and V.

The Dictionary 59
What Pupils now Know 59
The Teacher's Programme 60
Oral Methods 61
Exercise on the Camel 65
Exercise on the Elephant 68
Letter-Writing 70
Books of Authority on Topics Suitable for Language Exercise 72
Teachers' Consulting Library 74

HINTS ON LANGUAGE.

Grade I. — First Year.

LANGUAGE is the medium through which man communicates with his fellow. The degree of his culture is measured by the comparative fullness and precision with which he uses this medium. Not so much the possession of knowledge as the ability to impart it makes him valuable to society. To teach him to convey his ideas correctly is, then, as high a task as to teach him the ideas themselves. But the teacher of Grade I. has the double duty of creating ideas in her pupils' minds, and of calling out the correct expression of those ideas. Looked at broadly, it is not her business to teach her pupils to read or spell, to write or cipher, but to develop in them the correct use of the English language in its written or spoken forms. As the possession of ideas must precede the expression of them, the teacher will first endeavor to supply or create ideas in her pupils' minds. She does this through the operation of their senses, and in so

Language-teaching. — Its true place.

doing she merely introduces Nature's method into her schoolroom. Only in proportion as she makes herself Nature's assistant and interpreter will she succeed. As oral precedes written communication, her work in language will begin with oral communication; but whether oral or written, it must be considered first and last an exercise in language, of which reading, writing, spelling, and oral number-work are but the various forms.

The child enters school with the power of speech, and with a small vocabulary of words, sufficient to express, more or less perfectly, his ideas. To enlarge his vocabulary it is necessary to increase the number of his ideas. These will be obtained from objects, of which words are the symbols or representatives. Teach, therefore, no word until the idea it represents is understood; but, on the other hand, *make the symbol as familiar as the object.* As Nature presents objects as wholes, teach the symbols of these objects as wholes; then analyze the objects in point of form, color, size, and their symbols in point of sound. (New teachers sometimes think that because reading is no longer taught by analyzing words into their component letters, that the letters themselves are not to be taught; and a teacher of Grade I. once objected to receiving a pupil because he did not know his letters, as if it were not her business to teach them.)

As ideas are to be produced by means of objects, the objects must be shown. Talking about an object conveys no tangible idea to the child. To appreciate he must see. If the object itself cannot be shown, it should be represented by a picture. If the picture be not at hand, one should be drawn upon the board. The act of drawing is itself interesting, as line after line completes a recognizable form before a group of eager spectators. The teacher of Grade I. should be able to talk easily, and to draw. She should herself talk in order to excite ideas and expression in her pupils, and to draw in order to convey visible form when other representations are lacking.

Remember that your pupils, if left to themselves, would talk all the time. This tendency should not be repressed in Grade I., but directed into proper channels. In many cases the teach- *Talking as Language.* er's first duty is to overcome the timidity of certain children who find themselves in a strange room, surrounded perhaps by strangers, told to sit quietly in rows, facing a personage clothed with powers of, to them, vague and limitless authority. *Be mindful of first impressions.* A sunbeam from the teacher's heart may at once melt the child's soul into music like that of Memnon's statue; a cross or nervous welcome, a frown or threat, will freeze it into stone. A schoolroom of this grade, awed into silence, is more depressing than the " Street of the Tombs " in Pompeii. Talk to your children merrily and heartily, and make them talk,— first to remove their timidity, and then to enlarge their power of expression. Make them love to hear your voice, and your power over them will be unlimited.

Make all your talking, however, *tell*. With this in view begin with objects of daily life, familiar to all children. Show the picture of a cat, a dog, or a hen, or point to some object in the room, because the pupil will recognize the symbols of these objects sooner than those of objects hitherto unknown. Draw the picture of such objects as cannot be shown; talk about them and let the children talk. In order that the power of language thus gained may be readily applied to reading, a list of three hundred words is given on pages 31, 32 which are to be developed during the first five months of school life. This system will be pursued for two months at least, before any attempt is made to teach reading from print, because at least that length of time is necessary to provide a sufficient number of ideas clearly apprehended by the child's mind, and because it is only after such a probationary period that the symbols of those ideas, which we call words, will be also equally well defined and unmistakably impressed, so that the symbol for *cat* cannot by any misapprehension be applied to the idea *dog*. Let us enter a schoolroom and see how this system of development may be applied to a class recently admitted. The first lesson, for instance, is "a dog."

A group of eight or ten children run from their seats at the teacher's call, and surround her at the

Object Lessons in Language.

blackboard. No timidity is apparent, for they have become thoroughly acquainted with her before the lesson is attempted. She has in her mind the word to be developed, and knows how to *interest*, which is the first step. "How many can tell me what their eyes are for?" is her first question. "To see," "to look with." "Yes; now open them wide and look straight at me, and see what I am going to do." The class are all attention. With a few strokes of the crayon, and as rapidly as possible, the teacher draws the outline of a dog. Before it is finished the whispered words, "It's a dog! See the head! See the legs!" can be heard from the group. The children tell the teacher what it is, and a talk follows about dogs. The teacher asks what the dog says and does, and if they have one at home. She then writes the word on the board — "a dog" — and says "a dog." "I will put the word *a dog* on the board for every little boy and girl." Each child covers his word with his hand, and all say the word "a dog" in natural voice. Ask different children what word they have. *All* look at the word attentively, and then close their eyes and think how it looks. Finally ask them what they would do if a dog should come into school. "Laugh," says one. "Yes, probably, but should we let him stay?" "No, we would drive him away." "Well, then, I think we had better send *the dog* we have here away." All erase in great haste, and then the teacher tells the children to run to their seats

The Development Method.

and make a picture of a dog like the one on the board (later on they will be able to *copy* the new word).

We will now apply this method to a common idiom, like *I see, O see*. "How many can tell me once more, this afternoon, what they do with their eyes?" "Look, see, see!" "Yes, how do you know your teacher is here before you?" "We can see you." "Yes, what did you see right here on the board this morning?" "A dog." "Well, can you see a dog here now? No? Very well, look round the room and tell me what you can see." Teacher starts the game by saying, "*I* see a clock; I see a book." The children join in with, "I see a bell, I see a chair, I see you," etc. "Run to the window and tell me what you can see. Now what do you see here?" the teacher asks as they return, taking a toy dog from her pocket. "A dog! a dog!" "Yes, but tell me the *whole* story. When you were at the window you said '*I see a bird! I see a tree!*' Now what's the story about the dog?" "I see a dog," some one says. "Now I will write it on the board and all the children may say it over *once, twice, three* times." "I see a dog," is the response, as the teacher writes the word up very high on the board, down low, in a doghouse, etc. "Children, if we should go out into the hall, and should see a *real* dog, what do you think we should say?" "A dog's out there!" says one. "Perhaps so, but if you were *very* much surprised,

Margin note: I See, O See, Developed.

as you would be to see a *big, black dog* in the hall, I think you would make your mouth very round and say, 'O see the dog!'" Teacher makes *O see the dog* on the board. "Now, children, make believe you are surprised and say, 'O see the dog!'" Compare *O see* and *I see.* Let them take their seats and make a picture of something they can *see* in the room. Ask them when they go home to use their eyes and tell you whatever they may see on the way.

Let us now apply our method to teaching the symbol *Cat.* " How many are glad to come up here to see teacher this morning? Those who are may raise their hands; and, if you are very glad, you may raise *both* hands." "Good! Now how many remember what the story was about yesterday? Look at me and try very hard to think; now the one who thinks first may come here and whisper the word to me." All but two of the ten get the right word, and go to the place indicated, by the teacher's desk. Reward these children by letting them clap their hands vigorously for a few seconds, then let the one who thought first tell the word for the benefit of the two children who did not know. The teacher then writes the word *a dog* on the board several times, then the stories, *I see a dog.' O see a dog!* The children distinguish between the two, and different ones repeat the sentences. "How many remembered to use their eyes coming to school this morning?" A few tell what they saw, and then the teacher asks if they would like to know

A Cat.

what *she* saw on her way to school. "Well, I will tell you all about it, and I will see if you can guess what it was. As I was walking along, something came right out from behind a tree, and ran across the road. Now, it was about *so* long; it was *all* white, and had four legs and a long tail. What do you think it was?" "A dog, a hen, a cat," are the various answers. "Well, children, it looked to me very much like this;" and the teacher draws rapidly the picture of a cat running. (If the teacher cannot do this, she might tell the class to close their eyes while she gets a toy cat, a pasteboard representation of a cat, such as are very common as advertisements, or, as a last resort, she may show the picture of a cat, but be sure to show some representation of the real object, and if possible *draw it*.) Talk about the *cat* as about the *dog*, and write *a cat* under the picture. Write it many times, and let the children say "a cat." Then write the word in yellow, red, blue, green crayons. Let the pupils close their eyes; then hide the new word, *i. e.*, write it on different parts of the board, and at the same time write "a dog" to see if the children can distinguish one from the other. The new word may be written in a column of unfamiliar words, and the word "a cat" picked out. Finally, write the word in very large letters, and refer the children to it just before going home. Ask them to tell mamma about the new word they have learned. Of course, the idioms *I see*, *O see*, must be written in connection with a *cat*, and the stories "I see a dog," "I see a cat," compared. The word *rat* would naturally come next, and would be introduced when the story of the cat is reviewed and continued.

Let us now take the action word *ran*. The teacher says next morning. "Children, the cat that I told you about yesterday, and told you I had at home"—"I know, the one with the short tail," interrupts Johnnie. "Yes, Johnnie, that very one went down into the cellar last night, and what do you think she saw?" "Some rats," is the immediate answer. "Yes, now what do you suppose she did?" "Chased them!" says one. "Ran!" says another. "True, the cat ran and the rats ran. Now for a nice game! I am going to let Frank make believe he is a *cat*, because he is the largest boy, and all the rest may be rats. Now, then, the rats may start and run round the table, and the cat may run after them. Quick!" This is great fun, and the cat and rats start off at full speed. When they return they are bright and animated with the exercise. "Now, tell me quickly what you did just now." "We ran." "But the cat didn't catch me," says one "Yes, you all *ran*. Look, see what the chalk says,"—*ran, ran, ran* is written hastily on the board. All say the word over and over again. "Now, children, it says *I ran, I ran*, now *a cat ran, a dog ran*," etc. The teacher compares *rat* with *ran*, and then turning suddenly says: "Now, you may all run to your seats."

Ran.

After the words *a boy*, *a girl* have been taught, introduce a few familiar proper names — Frank, Tom, Max, Nell, Ann, etc. It is an easy matter after a few object and action words have been introduced to teach the quality words. A very *fat* pig can be drawn and compared with a *lean* one, a large hat with a small one, etc. If the teacher should tell a story about a boy who robbed a bird's nest, and then ask the question, Was he a *good* or a *bad* boy? the desired word would be almost surely spoken by the children.

We will now suppose all the words under the heading "First and Second Months" have been properly developed. The pupils have by this time a vocabulary of fifty-five words, and can tell them simply or in sentences. The lessons will now be conducted on a little different plan from that employed when only one or two words were known. At the end of the second month we will suppose the teacher to be again before her class. The children now know what these lessons are, and spring eagerly forward at the mention of Johnnie's or Nellie's class. Turning quickly to the board the teacher says : "We will have a story this morning about *a good boy* (the italicized words are put on the board and told by the class) of the name of Tom. This boy lived on a farm in the country. Now, he had a great many things to do: he had a *fat pig*, *an old red cow*, *a white hen* and *some chicks*, and *a big ox* to feed and take care of

Review.

every day. One day he took a walk into the woods with *a little girl.* Who do you think she was? Yes, his sister, and she took her *doll* with her, and a *large fan,* too, for it was very warm. "Their *little dog* Jip went with them, and did a great many funny things. They saw *a sly fox,* and Jip *ran* after him for a long way," etc. And so the story might continue until all the words are brought in. The next day an entirely different story may be told. This, however, is only one of the many ways of reviewing the words. They may fill the rounds of a *red* ladder, be packed into a *blue* trunk, or put into a basket, or, what is still more interesting, be hung on the branches of a Christmas tree. Aim to give the children a variety of exercise ; try to do something different in each lesson.

In the "third month" the words are a little more difficult, but the ideas they express are still familiar. Many of these *object* words would naturally come into the same story. Frank might catch *a fish* in *the pond,* and put it into *a pail.* A *frog* might jump into the *water,* a *ship, swan,* or *duck* might be seen on the water, etc. At the end of the second month the child is able to begin to read from the chart ; during the third month he can read the first half. The printed words must be compared with the script, so that at the end of the third month the class will be able to put into script on their slates the printed stories on the chart. When this is done much will have been accomplished, and the class

Third Month.

will take up the book at the beginning of the fourth month with little difficulty.

Writing. During the progress of the development method in teaching reading and language at the same time, the pupil is learning to write. Begin on his entrance to school with the letters composed of the simplest strokes, like *u* and *n*, *i* and *e*, written on slates ruled with lines not less than a quarter of an inch apart. Teach a large round hand. It can hardly be too large to overcome the pupil's tendency to write a small contracted hand. Before the words of the "first and second months" are developed, the pupil will be able to write them, certainly the simplest of them. When the chart is taken, he will write most of its sentences, at least two or three of each page. Teach also as early as possible the capitals A, which begins an army of sentences, and I. As soon as the script words of the board are compared with printed words upon the chart, teach the pupil to connect the two in their minds, and note their correspondence and differences. Teach the class to hold the slate pencil exactly as you would teach them to hold a pen if you were teaching penmanship. See that the slates lie upon the desks, and do not rest on the child's lap and the edge of the desk. Write a copy for the class on the board in a round hand, more carefully executed than is possible in the hurried manner of developing words. Let the class practice the use of crayon on the board, and in such exercise teach an easy swinging method of making curves, ovals, and circles. Continue this in higher grades, to counteract the cramping tendency of copy-books and paper, where pupils think they must be particular and so hold the pen as in a vice, with effects fatal to freedom and elasticity. When your other duties permit, see how the class write by looking at their work when it is in progress. Continue this inspection in all grades, and do not let your pupils learn to apply the proverb of the Russian peasants to excuse their shiftlessness: "Heaven is high and the czar afar off." Gradually, as the year goes on, the first grade will learn to write all that they read. Make this the end and aim of your work in writing, which should be to connect it with and make it a part of reading and language-exercise, or rather, one of the departments of the development of language in the pupils committed to your care. To teach children to read what, after a proper time, they cannot write, is like a boy walking on stilts of unequal length.

The child has now been taught to read, through the medium of language-exercises of the most important character. Not only has he gained a large number of ideas and found symbols **Reading.** for their expression, but he has prepared himself to apply to oral expression those symbols when printed, which we call reading.

Having been taught to talk easily and naturally he reads naturally, and as if he were talking. From this time the teacher's task is easy, and reading becomes as natural an exercise as talking. A sentence with the question-mark presents no difficulty, because the pupil was taught to modulate his inflection in asking a question while he was engaged in the development-work upon the board. In reading from the chart do not point to words separately, or one by one. That habit causes the pupil to merely pronounce the individual words of a sentence, — *I-see-a-cat*, — which is not reading. Let the pupil read each sentence silently, then aloud as a whole. The success of your entire year, and that of teachers to follow you, depends upon a direction so simple and yet so necessary. When, however, your pupils have read the chart intelligently, they are ready, at the end of the fourth month, to take a book, and the work of language-exercise goes on under new conditions, but on the same principles and with similar results.

When the book is to be introduced, call a squad into the floor and hand them the primers from your desk. They will thank you for them as for any gift. Select the new words, and put the first one on the board. If none know it, tell its name and meaning. Place it in a sentence, or let the children do so. Do not tell the new word if they can discover it themselves. Suppose the first sentence is: "The bird sits on the branch of the tree." All the words but *branch* you know to be familiar to the class. Ask where the bird is. "On the tree," some will say.

"Yes, but on what part of the tree?" "On the limb, branch, twig," will be the various answers. If the word *branch* does not appear, draw a tree and teach the new word from the picture. Let the class find the new word in the lesson. When they take their seats they will write such words more than once. When on the floor, teach them to talk in such a way as to bring in the new words. Do not lose sight of the fact that the reading-lesson, like all your work, is a language-exercise; and develop new words in the book in the same manner as those on the card. Ask pupils questions which can be answered by short sentences. Avoid such as may be answered by merely *yes* or *no*, or by a repetition of the thought of the question. So, in higher grades, do not recite the pupil's lessons for him, leaving him to approve of your statements by a monosyllable.

See that every pupil reads each sentence silently. Then let each *out of turn* read a sentence. Then let the story be read in turn from the beginning. Each pupil thus reads the whole story silently for the thought, and two sentences at least for oral expression. When that is done let the class close books and tell the story. They can then run to their seats and write what they can remember, or such sentences as the teacher may prescribe. Let them recall the story of the previous day, and write it in their own language.

Teach all words phonetically, and use diacritical marks at your discretion. Phonic drill tends to

open the mouth, a very important habit. Each word
Phonic Ex- when taught should be distinctly pronounced
ercise. by the teacher, making each sound separately. The class must then imitate her. Train them to open the mouth from the first day. Timidity on entering school closes the mouth, and confirmed bad habit produces mumbling. First make children feel at home, then make them speak distinctly. In all grades make them look at you when they recite, and not at the window. The seeds of bad habits of enunciation and recitation in grammar grades are sown in the first years of school life.

Do not allow the child in reading to say *thŭgh-
book*, *ŭgh-cat*. This is not a part of the "New
Thŭgh- Education," although new teachers have
book. done that system great injustice by suppos-
Ŭgh-cat. ing it to consist in substituting *thŭgh-book* for *the-book*, and *ŭgh-cat* for *a-cat*. Neither is correct; nor is *thŭgh* pronounced separately any improvement upon *the*. The proper pronunciation is that suggested in the "Manual of the Board of Education" of New York City: When the child reads *the* in a sentence, as, *See the cat and the dog play*, let him pronounce it with the following word, as if it formed the first syllable of that word, speaking *the* lightly as [e] in the words *e-vent'*, *e-vade'*. The *a*, when used as a word in like circumstances, should be pronounced like *a* in *a-muse'*.

Language has hitherto been considered in connection with reading; but language lessons as such should simultaneously form a part of every day's work. They begin with a child's entrance to school: for "making him talk" is but a language lesson in disguise. These lessons have as objects operation of the senses, quickening of the imagination, proper expression of ideas gained by the senses, the use of new idioms, etc. They are to be given to a squad of ten or twelve, not to the whole school. The time of each lesson will be about fifteen minutes. The manner and style in which these lessons are given, and their results, will largely depend upon each teacher's originality. The following hints may be useful: Present a picture, and let the children look at it closely. Ask them to tell you what they see. Be sure everything is mentioned, and in complete sentences, as, *I see a dog,* not *a dog, a cat.* Then lead them on by saying: "I think the dog will catch the cat." They will naturally follow by: "I think the cat will climb the tree," etc. Aid pupils by the use of the interrogatives *who, which, what, where, what kind, how many, why.* Children should give sentences including all the objects in the picture, their color and position, what they are, where they have been, what they are doing, or have been doing, what they are made of (if animals, their habits, uses, etc.). If children are represented, let the class give their names, where they live, what they probably have at home, etc. Pupils find difficulty in learning and properly using brief idiomatic expressions. They may best be taught by picture lessons. The following should constantly be brought in and spoken so many times that they become perfectly familiar : *This is, it is, here is, there are, she has, they have, I think, I see*, etc. Give several lessons from one picture. In the first, note in a general way all the objects in the picture, the names of which may be written on the board. Next notice the quality, color (if animals, their habits and uses) ; thirdly, the position, what they are doing, where they are going, etc. In each successive lesson on the picture, review all that has been said before. The following exercise was given by a teacher during the latter part of the first year. One day she took a picture representing an old sheep and a lamb. A tall girl with a red dress was giving the sheep some grass from her hand, while a large boy was holding his baby brother on the sheep's back. The baby had a long stick in his hand, and his hat (yellow) was on the ground. The children were apparently in the field, and the house, barn, trees, fence could be seen in the distance. The class spent about ten minutes in the morning talking about the picture, noticing the objects in it in point of color and size, and the following words were written on the board near the picture : *old sheep, sheep's back, little lamb, brother, baby boy, whip, hand, tall girl, red dress, yellow hat, green grass, barn, field, house, trees.* Many of these words were familiar to the children ; nevertheless they were all written, and were copied several times until the pupils' slates were full. The words were then erased, and in the afternoon the class wrote the names of all the objects they could see in the picture from memory. They wrote correctly most of the words they had copied in the morning. They were familiar with all the idioms referred to elsewhere (*this is, it is*, etc.), so that in the afternoon they wrote stories about the objects they could see in the picture, and such sentences as the following were produced : " Here is an old sheep and a little lamb." " I see a baby on the sheep's back." " He has a long whip." " I see the brother." " He is a great boy." " This is a good girl." " She has some green grass." " She has a red dress on." " I see the yellow hat." " I see the barn." " I see the house." " They are in the field." These were disconnected, but in almost every case correct, beginning with a capital and ending with a period. The teacher copied such sentences as could be used later, and the stories were erased. The next day, when the teacher suggested another talk about the picture, all were interested and eager. Having noted the *objects* in the picture, the class were ready to talk about the *story* it contained. They were told to look at the picture for a few moments, and *think* what the children were doing, what their names were, etc. In less than a minute every hand was up, and these stories were given *orally* in quick succession : " I think the big boy's name is Frank and the little boy's name is Johnnie." " Frank is giving his baby brother a ride." "Johnnie likes to sit on the sheep's back, it is so soft." "Nell is feeding the old sheep." "The little lamb is hungry, too." "The little boy has a whip in his hand; I think he will hit the sheep." "The little boy's hat has fallen off." "I think they all live in that house." "When it is night the sheep and the lamb will go into the barn." Many more sentences are given, and, the ten minutes having expired, the teacher tells the children to take their seats and write all the stories they have told, *everything they can think of about* the picture. The teacher wrote on the board such words as they had used in their oral stories and were unable to write, but which they would need to use in writing: viz., *Frank, Johnnie, Nellie, sheep's back, giving, feeding, ride, soft, fallen, live, night,* etc., and promised to write any other words called for. When the slates were examined half an hour later, nearly all the stories told orally were written. The best sentences are put on paper by the teacher, and the slate-work is erased.

The next day the teacher asked the class of what use the sheep was, and a long talk followed. Some one knew that the flesh was good for food, another had ideas on the wool which grows on the sheep's back. They were told how sheep are washed and sheared, and the wool put into bags and sent to mills in Clinton and woven into cloth by the parents of some of the class. A piece of wool was shown, and the boys were told that their jackets were made of it. The children were much interested, and gained some information, but they were unable to write many stories, their vocabulary not being large enough to enable them to write a composition on *Wool.* Such short sentences were obtained as: "There is wool on the sheep's back." "It is thick, it is soft, it is warm." "We make cloth of it." "My coat has wool in it." "The wool will keep us warm." But when the teacher questioned them the next day, they remembered all they had been told. For a final lesson a review was made of all the previous lessons, and the following story was written on the board for the children to read over and copy accurately. *This story is composed entirely of the children's best sentences,* which were taken down by the teacher when the lessons were given, and the class so understood it. As the teacher wrote the first story, she said: "This story I found on Mary's slate; who can read it?" and so on: —

Here is an old sheep and a little lamb. There is wool on the sheep's back. It is soft and white. I think the large boy's name is Frank. He is giving the little boy a ride. His name is Johnnie. I think Johnnie likes to ride on the sheep's back. He will not fall off. He has a whip in his hand. He will hit the old sheep. The little boy's hat fell off. I can see Nellie. She is feeding the old sheep. She is a good girl. She has a red dress on. She will give the lamb some grass. They are in the field. Frank will put the sheep and the lamb in the barn at night. I should like to have a little lamb.   **The Story.**

Simple lessons on the domestic animals furnish an excellent subject for language-exercise.

Take the cat, for instance. Ask the children to name and tell you about its different parts. If all the teacher gets from them is merely *I see the ears, I see the feet*, etc., the lesson will be of but little use; but if the teacher should ask if the cat's eyes are different from ours, tell them to notice her eyes when the sun shines or when it is dark, explain how and why she sees in the dark, call attention to the sharply-curved pins in her cushioned paws, ask what she does when she is happy or irritated, notice the rough tongue, call out the sly, furtive habit of approaching her prey, and her deceptive amiability; the cat will be invested with a new interest in the child's mind, and will undergo thorough inspection at home. In all this do not tell them anything they can discover as facts for themselves. Make a list of animals, grouping those with hoofs, with horns, etc., and write down a brief synopsis of their uses, habits, whether wild or domestic, where found, how caught, how tamed. Not less than in higher grades is preparation necessary in Grade I. for a proper presentation of the subject-matter of instruction.

<small>The Cat as Object Lesson.</small>

In addition to these special language lessons, certain general exercises should be given once or twice a week during the first three or four months of school life. They should be short, occupying five or six minutes, and should include the entire school. The purpose of these lessons is to bring children to talk freely, to observe closely

<small>General Exercises.</small>

what they see, and to be able to describe it, and to bring out original sentences from all. Take the children as soon as they come in from the playground. Ask one who is apt to talk what he has been doing. His description of some game he has engaged in will lead others to join in the conversation, unconsciously. Ask the children when they say good-by to remember to tell something next session that they saw on their way home, the color, size, etc. As the subject of another conversation ask how they spent the last holiday; ask them if they have ever been to Boston, New York, to the nearest city, into the country, or to the seashore. Let them tell their experiences, what they did or saw. By asking questions bring them to tell what they have at home, their pets, playthings, and about the baby. Let them put their heads down on their desks and dream, then rise and relate their dreams. This cultivates their imaginative as well as conversational powers. Perform some act, or let the children do so. Some one will be called upon to tell what was done, in such sentences as: " You opened the window and shut the blinds." "James took a block and put it on John's desk." Let them think of everything that can run, fly, hop, etc. " A bird can fly." " A cat can run." Try guessing and thinking games. Suggest to the children that they make pictures on their slates, giving each row a subject. At the close of the session let the one who has the best picture tell all about it. Tell some interesting story, illustrating it by drawing as you proceed; then call upon them to repeat the story next day. Give the children little cards with one object-word written upon each, and let them make sentences with that word in them. Put a list of words on the board; let the children rise, and each give a sentence with one of those words in it.

Endeavor to make all their lessons in drawing, clay-modelling, color, and number, language lessons, requiring the pupil to give complete answers: *This is a sphere. It is perfectly round. Three blocks and four blocks are seven blocks. My stick is yellow. If you put blue and yellow together you will have green color.*

VOCABULARY OF WORDS.

This vocabulary contains three hundred words to be developed during the first five months (twenty weeks) of school life. The following words are not included, being taught or pronounced with object-words: *a, an, the,* and such idioms as, *this is, it is, I have, I see, I think, can you, who has, let me,* etc.

Object-words may be changed to their plural form and a few proper names added from time to time. Use frequently the question-mark. Make reviews by constantly repeating words already learned in connection with new ones.

Words preceded by the asterisk are to be taught by association in sentences.

Vocabulary of Words.

First and Second Months.

Rat, cat, mat, hat, boy, girl, man, fan, pan, top, ball, hen, pig, cow, bell, mug, tub, kid, dog, doll, hay, cup, cap, egg, bird, bee, ox, box, fox.

See, ran, hit, sat, catch, get, fed, spin, eat, lay, fly.

White, red, fat, big, little, pretty, old, sly, good.

* Yes, no, not, and, at, on.

Third Month.

Horse, oats, lamb, chair, ship, fish, dish, swan, pond, duck, book, corn, nuts, nest, tree, chick, kitten, milk, cake, frog, water, pail, cage, rabbit, basket, grass, bush, rose, branch, hill.

Lie, look, play, sing, jump, go, lap, put, build.

Blue, black, happy, small, large, bad, new, one, two, three, four, long, tall.

* Where, very, how, but, for, to, in, with.

Fourth Month.

Sister, brother, boat, lake, slate, desk, door, house, floor, mouse, trap, eye, face, cheek, mouth, nose, hand, morning, night, goat, kite, tail, string, school, home, cart, worm, glass, dress, coat, name, game, bear, paw, bread, apple, spool, robin, crow, wing.

Beg, buy, fall, take, ask, stand, give, work, love, write, read, hide, make, row, come, drink, ride, walk, stop, drop, help, hatch.

Green, nice, funny, warm, poor, five, six, seven, some, bright, sweet, brave, tame.

* After, if, that, when, here, from, too, please, wish, thank.

Fifth Month.

Sheep, horn, farm, barn, teacher, papa, mamma, baby, wool, wood, stove, candy, snow, wagon, pony, stick, summer, winter, drum, sled, playthings, shell, sand, plant, leaf, flower, picture, sun, head, ear, chin, hair, clothes, flag, boot, clock, ground, knife, fork, spoon, plate, lamp, child, friend, lady, rain.

Help, slide, carry, draw, hold, keep, bring, meet, hear, grow, tell, strike, swim, throw, buzz, count, drive, stay, find, hope, shine.

Polite, best, kind, cross, young, great, any, eight, nine, ten, cold, yellow, brown, dear, pleasant, hard, soft, sick, dark, every, still, glad, fast, merry.

* Always, well, out, much, over, into, down, then, there.

Grade II.— Second Year.

Read carefully the preceding pages. Much of them concerns your work. The pupils of Grade I. have during the year, since their entrance to school, developed the words on the card, read the chart and all the primers in the market at sight. They are now ready to enter Grade II., and continue their growth in language in more extended form. They have learned to read, and read correctly because understandingly, in Grade I. From this time on, reading is only practice in whatever grade it may occur. The method is not different, at least until Grade IV. is reached. New words are taught in the same manner in Grades II. and III. as in Grade I. The class come into the floor without having seen the lesson, and are eager to read a new story. If they had studied their lesson they would read it with no interest, any more than adults would read a novel with interest the second time in the same day. There is not on this subject one rule for the man and another for the child, but in the tertiary period of education it was not thought necessary that children should be interested in what they read. If it were only "good," and they read it without stumbling, it was enough. But, on the other hand, sight-reading, as we have defined it, kills machine reading. It is no more necessary for a primarian to study his reading lesson (competent instruction being always presupposed) than it is for an adult to study the newspaper he intends to read to his family. In either case there may be a word he does not know. The adult consults his dictionary, the primarian his teacher. The difference is only in the source of information.

The teacher may ask a few questions about the picture which accompanies the lesson, but not to a great extent, for when the book is read at sight such questions are properly review questions. It will be better for her to say, "We are

Reading.

going to read about a picnic the children had in a grove near the house. I must first teach you a word or two that you may better enjoy the story." Write such on the board. Let each child find the print word in the book corresponding to the script word on the board, and point to it, pronouncing it. The teacher explains the word, or, better, she draws its meaning from the class. Make each word as familiar to the child as the picture or object is, and explain quality and action words as in Grade I. Let the pupils read each sentence silently, and do not divide sentences if possible, thereby letting the voice fall before the idea is complete. (Hence in Grade II., as in Grade I., only simple sentences should be used; the semi-colon, and compound and complex sentences belong to Grade III.) Struggle against the habit or inclination of dropping the voice at a comma. In some schools this is a universal blemish in reading. If not overcome in Grade II., where commas are properly introduced into reading-books, it will disfigure all subsequent attempts to read. Call upon pupils out of turn to read sentence by sentence. If one pupil does not use correct expression, emphasis, or inflection, call upon a second or third until you obtain it. That is better than suggesting it, but when once discovered the teacher may dwell upon it, and call upon the class to repeat the phrase or sentence correctly. Beware of much recitation in common, however. It is a relic of the machine. It helps ignorance hide its deficiency by silence. It is particularly odious in oral spelling, as it begets a sing-song and listless enunciation. Have the story read through a second time, as in Grade I. Call for synonyms in the case of new or difficult words, especially quality or action words. Opening a second reader at random, we find such words as *hovered, darted, flaxen, peevish, coward, murmured, grandly, puzzled, uncoil, quivered, powdered, delicate, prisoner, civil, ruffled, tiny, cunning, sniffed, timidly.* These words need explanation from the teacher, because no amount of "study" at his seat would give a child of six or seven years an idea of the shade of meaning suggested by the word "quivered" or "murmured." And on the other hand to tell him the words, that is, to pronounce them for the pupil, teaches him neither the idea nor its symbol. It only supplies for the moment the missing link in a chain of disconnected words. Nevertheless such so-called "study," supplemented when it failed, as it did constantly, by the teacher pronouncing the word, was once considered sufficient to produce good readers. Nor is sight-reading, literally interpreted, any better. To put a book into a child's hand and tell him to read for the first time any piece without the slightest preparation is as sensible as to ask a blind man to describe the paintings in a picture gallery. True sight-reading is the continuation in higher grades of the development method of the list of words, illustrated in the work of Grade I. The instruction necessary to attach an idea to otherwise meaningless symbols is a language-exercise. Look upon it as such, and reflect that it gives the reading exercise its chief value. Sight-reading, using that term always in the sense of a development exercise, allows opportunity for practice in language which would be impossible if pupils only came into the floor to read what they had previously studied, and knew by heart, with the exception of certain words to be told by the teacher. But legitimate sight-reading as an aid to the development of language, and language-exercise as a help to reading, take the pupil hand in hand through this and each succeeding grade.

Do not, therefore, in this or any grade, tell a pupil to spell a word over which he stumbles. That may give him the pronunciation, although it is hard to show how his saying *see-a-tee* suggests the pronunciation *cat*. Remember that it is not pronunciation you are now looking for, but thought. The idea will call out the word. The word will not suggest the idea, otherwise he would not have stumbled. Apply the development method in any grade, and the reading thus produced is sight-reading, and sight-reading is true reading, the only reading worthy of the name. It is not supplanted by study until the pupil is old enough to develop the thought himself assisted by a dictionary.

Do not ask the meaning of a single word, or attempt to define it, if it is part of a phrase, or if it requires some other word in the text to complete

SPELLING. 37

its meaning. Define two or more words together if they are closely connected. Avoid technical definitions, but when it is necessary to give one, let it be brief, compact, and complete. Beware of loose definitions, and do not use the word you are defining or any part of it: as, *Definition is defining a word.* Such a definition only moves you in a circle. In this grade begin to call for words of similar sound but of dissimilar meaning. Use sentences containing such words, and call attention to any differences in spelling. "There" and "their" are sources of frequent confusion. *Tail* and *tale, leaves, scent, close,* (also "*clothes*" mispronounced), *hair* and *hare, bear, sew, left, here, right,* are but a few which will occur to the teacher. **Definition.**

When the whole story has been read call upon each scholar for a sentence from it, of original form if possible. You will find that after the three readings described above, the class will know the entire story, and be able to tell it.

Separate spelling from reading. Do not remove the impression of the story by a mechanical exercise. When the piece is read, let the squad on going to their seats write the abstract of it, such as they may have already given orally. In the meantime the next squad comes out and takes the books. (Hence, when the town or city owns the books, a dozen copies will equip a class with reading material.) Make spelling a separate exercise. Do not in any grade think your pupils will under- **Spelling.**

stand a word by merely spelling it. If that were so, dictionaries would be unnecessary. Spelling teaches pronunciation, but reading has ceased, or ought to cease, to be a pronouncing exercise. Oral spelling should aim at producing clear enunciation and correct pronunciation. Each word should be pronounced by the pupil before and after spelling, but spelling by syllables is obsolete. It is well, however, for pupils to divide the word into syllables mentally, making a slight pause between each. Oral spelling should be a review of the week's written work. It should be largely occupied with words spelled incorrectly during that time. Such mistakes may be noticed by writing them on the board, calling attention to them and then erasing them. Let no incorrect word remain longer on the board in any grade than is necessary for correction. "When seen too oft," it may delude into permanent error.

Language. The language-work in Grade II. is written, just as most of that of Grade I. is oral. It is first written on slates, then transferred to ruled paper. In the early part of the year, when many new words are presented to the children, an exercise like the following may be beneficial. Write upon the board ten or more new words which have been developed during the reading lesson, and let the class put them into sentences. The following words may serve as an illustration: *robin, away, thank, send, eel, swan, jump, happy, mill, almost.* When the class has given the following sentences orally, the teacher will write them on the board: "The robin sings sweetly." "I am going away to-night." "I thank my mother when she gives me something to eat." "My sister will send me to the store after school." "An eel is a funny fish." "A swan has a long neck." "I can jump over a stone wall." "I am a happy little girl." "My father works in the mill." "I was almost late at school this morning." Let the class copy these sentences on their slates; and then call upon different members to read them. In all such cases reject incomplete sentences, or such as merely bring in the required word with one or two others. Children naturally compose short sentences, but as their ideas expand their expression of them should be gradually developed. The teacher says: "Give me a sentence containing the word *discouraged*." "I am discouraged," says a boy. That may be true, but the idea is incomplete, however perfect the sentence may be. No one can be *discouraged* without a cause for discouragement. Therefore a sentence which shall contain this word and be fully expressed should be given in such form as this: "I am discouraged because I cannot read as well as Mary."

Pictures play an even more important part in this grade than in Grade I. because the work to be done with them is capable of greater development. Every teacher should make a large collection of good pictures. They may be cut out of illustrated papers and pasted on stout cardboard. Pictures of animals are among those

Picture Lessons.

most successfully employed. In giving a lesson to a class on this subject, begin by taking any of the domestic animals, as all children are more or less familiar with them, and will therefore talk more freely and intelligently about them. Remember that in these exercises you are endeavoring to expand the pupil's power of expression. You do this by exciting him to talk, not by talking yourself. This is true of language-work in all grades. With young children a teacher should limit herself at first to the most obvious and best known features of animals, and gradually extend her range of instruction as her pupils are prepared for it. The following lesson on *the cow* was given to a class during the first month of the second year. Two lessons were required to complete the exercises, the first being devoted to oral expression and to copying all new words by the class, the second to written work. A large picture of a cow was procured, one that the class could easily see (or the animal may be sketched on the blackboard). Words suggestive of the different parts to be talked about, as Head, Neck, Horns, Tail, Teeth, Hoofs, etc., were written around the picture. The class were asked if any of them had ever noticed a peculiar habit which cattle have when standing in the barnyard, or when lying down after feeding. As no one seemed to know what was referred to, the teacher told them about the cow chewing the cud. Then a talk followed about the hoofs. The horse's hoofs were said to be whole, but a cow's are divided. The class were shown a picture of a cow's hoof. They were told that a cow rises upon her hind feet first. The several uses of the cow were then brought out, but nothing was written in this lesson. The next day the following was written by the class upon their slates from the previous day's conversation : —

The cow has a large head, short neck, and long tail. She has two horns on her head. She has no front teeth on her upper jaw. The color of the cow is usually red, black, or spotted. Cows, like horses, have hoofs, but the hoofs of the cow are divided, in horses they are whole. The cow eats grass and hay. When cows lie down after feeding they chew their food. This is called chewing the cud. The cow gives us good sweet milk. From her milk we make butter and cheese. Her flesh we use for food. Leather for our boots and shoes is made from her hide. Her horns are used for making combs. Glue is made from her hoofs. Mortar is made with her hair. Her bones will be made into the handles of knives. A cow always gets up on her hind feet first.

This exercise may either be written by the class on their slates from memory, and then corrected in spelling, punctuation, capitalization, etc., or the teacher may write the story on the board and the class will copy it on their slates. Gradually, however, they should be brought to compose, so that their work may not become exclusively a copy of the teacher's writing. Faulty sentences given by pupils to be copied on the board and written on slates should be corrected at once, or a second or third pupil should be called upon to improve upon the mistakes of the first.

Let pupils in Grade II. write what they gave **orally** in Grade I., accounts of visits, synopses of stories they have read, or that have been told or read to them. Plants in the schoolroom are very good sources of language lessons.

The following is a short, original description of a picture, written by a pupil of Grade II. : —

Rose and Lulu have come to the spring to get some water. They have a pitcher and a pail to get the water in. Rose has picked a bouqet (*sic*). I think the water in the spring is very cool. Rose is standing and Lulu is sitting on a stone. They live in a house not far from the spring. I think they are getting the water for their mamma.   O. W.

The following description of a visit to the sea-shore is inserted exactly as it was written by a pupil of Grade II., as an exercise in composition : —

I went to Lynn beach last summer. I had a very nice time. On the water I saw a good many ships. I picked up a great many little shells. I found one big shell and I gave it to my cousin who was with me, and she put all her little shells in it. I brought home all the shells that I found. We walked all around the sea-shore. I liked to see the tide come in. We took off our shoes and stockings and paddled in the sea. We stayed only one day.   K. J.

As the number-work in Grade I. will include some notice of bodily organs, like hands, feet, toes, fingers, eyes, ears, etc., continue this in Grade II., and lay the foundation of that knowledge of physiology and hygiene now required in many States by law.

Letter-writing can be profitably begun in the second year, and forms an interesting diversion as well as a practical exercise. Children are interested in whatever seems to be real; and if they can send their letter to the person addressed, their satisfaction is increased. The following letter was delivered to me by a pupil of Grade II. It was written on ruled paper with a lead-pencil : —

Letter-Writing.

Clinton, June 22, 1885.

Dear Mr. Bent, — We had a good time at the picnic. We went in the morning, and we had five swings. At noon my sister, my mother, father, and my little brother came. We had a boat-ride for nothing. Why didn't you go? You would have had a nice time.

Good by.   v. w.

The author of this letter had learned in her second school year how to begin a letter, compose and end it with a child's expression. All that may follow from this time on will be but practice on a larger model. Notice the use of the hyphen, and of other marks of punctuation. Those included in this letter, together with the surprise mark, complete the punctuation of Grade II. They have seen the sign of the possessive case used in Grade I., and will copy it from the teacher's work on the board. Teachers must be satisfied with short letters on such subjects as school, what pupils do Saturdays, the games they play at recess, etc. The statements will be crude at first, and will be confined to a narrow range of topics. When those are exhausted give them easy subjects, and insist upon their keeping to them. Correct ungrammatical forms of speech used by your pupils, without giving any reasons therefor. As a rule, let no error go uncorrected. Do not, therefore, give out more work than you can correct, nor correct it when all interest in the subject-matter is lost. If you cannot correct all the compositions or exercises, let each scholar correct another's; but beware of trusting too much to this. It is not probable that your class can do your work for you successfully. Were this the case, you would be no longer indispensable. Do not, then, rely on pupils' corrections of errors. The common and odious forms of incorrect expression would be generally passed over by them, because perfectly natural and too familiar. You must wage a constant warfare against such vulgarisms as the following: *ain't, 'taint, got to* for *must, he don't* (how would *he do not* sound?), *lots of, he done, hain't got no, be you, I seen, was you, me and John, he gave Frank and I,* etc., together with whatever errors of speech may be common to your particular locality. Do not think it necessary to give the reason why particular forms of speech are incorrect or vulgar. Teachers stand in the place of parents, who are never obliged to give a reason for a command or prohibition. Much must be told as truth in all grades, the reason of which would be inappreciable to pupils. Above all things, set a good example of correct speech in your own conversation with your class, and beware of giving them an opportunity of correcting in

Correct Speech.

you what you have been endeavoring at other times to correct in them.

Dictation. In dictated language lessons read the story in your best voice, and read it but once. Let the children repeat each sentence after you before writing it. See that each child writes very slowly and carefully, entirely independently of his neighbor. Walk through the aisles, and notice how pupils hold their pencils. Correct on the spot all improper manipulation. Use long pencils. When they are more than half used take new ones. Never let children twist their fingers around stubs. Never allow anything but the pupil's best and correct effort to be transferred from slate to paper.

Number. Number lessons should be language-exercises as in Grade I., and so in all grades not using a book. It may be necessary to use objects at first; but gradually accustom pupils to think out processes, or learn mathematical facts independent of association with objects. The power of association, as has been said of literature as a profession, "is a good staff, but a bad crutch." Begin in Grade II. to throw away the crutch of object-lessons in number. Teach numbers from ten to twenty or thirty, so that all their possible combinations will present themselves without hesitation as facts as soon as called for, with a certainty that three sevens are twenty-one, and cannot by any possibility be twenty or twenty-two. If this is not thoroughly learned in Grade II., it will be necessary for some other teacher to do your work for you. Be careful to do your own work thoroughly, and do not attempt the next teacher's. Sufficient unto the grade is the work thereof. You will never be in danger of teaching what belongs to you too well.

Do not, on the other hand, make number-work too abstract. Children like to "keep store." Enliven number-work by concrete examples given by pupils. See that the sentences used are correct and the mathematical combinations possible. Do not in this or any other grade "multiply cats by dogs." The combinations of abstract numbers are always abstract. In multiplication the multiplier must be abstract, and in division the divisor. The product will be of the same kind as the multiplicand, and the quotient like the dividend. Dollars divided by dollars will not give sheep, so that it is better in all grades to apply concrete expressions, by way of explanation, to the result of abstract operation. That the class may be supplied with concrete examples when their own stock is exhausted, teachers should have upon their desks several primary arithmetics composed of practical every-day examples. When the teacher puts an example to the class, the answer should be a number simply, without repetition of the problem, but the examples given by pupils should be fully and correctly expressed by them. In one case you are calling for a mathematical fact, in the other for a language-exercise in mathematical form. The more you develop

Abstract and Concrete.

this power of expression, the greater scope and play you give to the imagination and the thinking powers. In no other subject is it possible to lead children to do, to talk, and to think, as in number.

Grade III. — Third Year.

In this grade the pupil begins to write with pen and ink. The careful formation of letters, which has been studied hitherto with slate and lead-pencils, will have sufficiently engrossed his attention without diverting it to a substance requiring special care like ink. It is claimed that writing with pencils, as pencils are generally held, promotes a cramped and awkward method of holding the pen. If that be so, it is the teacher's fault. Teach pupils to hold long pencils as they will later hold a penholder. A child can be taught to hold a slate-pencil when he enters school exactly as the teacher wishes him to hold it, and the lead-pencil follows the custom set the first year with the slate-pencil.

As the pupil begins to write with ink it is convenient to supply him with a writing-book, and the book should be ruled to correspond with the paper on which he will write his language-exercises. Most systems of books do not sufficiently regard the great progress which has been made in the amount of

Ink.

writing done during the early years of school life, so that the pupil is in advance of the system, and the amount of writing in a book intended to last six months or a year is ridiculously small in comparison with that accomplished every week in language-work under the supervision of progressive school authorities. But here, as in all departments, it is the teacher with a large, round, plain, unflourishing hand who will "set the copy" for the youthful penmen of to-day. To insure uniformity in the ascending grades it will be advisable to have a chart hung in all rooms as a direction to the eye, but it is "practice, and again practice, and always practice," which makes good writers, not systems, charts, or copy-books. Freedom in the play of the hand and arm is apt to yield to a cramped fashion of using books with their measured strokes and mathematical precision. Paint two or three slope lines across as many horizontal lines on the blackboard, and your writing book is a permanent fixture. Let children write capital letters upon it, to gain a free sweep of the hand, and see that the position of writing at their desks gives ample play to the fore-arm.

The language-work in Grade III. under the new conditions of pen and ink assumes greater import-

Reading and Number. ance, just as the power of expression has been expanding by means of the practice of the two preceding years. You will see by reading the work of these years that pupils are ready to write a letter, tell a story, or keep a store. The work of each year is a development of that already passed. As the pupil's powers are larger, so the field of operation is more extended. The employment of reading and number-work as a branch of language-exercise has been sufficiently dwelt upon. Reading is still the oral expression of what has been silently mastered. In Grades II. and III., classes will read all the books put into their hands,—at least six each year. Number-work is concerned with tables, with addition into hundreds' place, and corresponding subtraction. Add to this, for recreation in concrete calculation and mental arithmetic, the simplest tables of money, weights, and measures. Alternate the abstract and concrete forms of operations in this way, and continue the use of tables for mental exercise after taking up the written work of Grades IV. and V.

In order to give due importance to language-exercise, and to include all its forms, it may be well to make a programme of work extending through the week, each day to have its own peculiar exercise. **Language.** Twenty-five minutes will be time enough to give to language lessons in this grade. Fifteen or twenty minutes may be occupied by pupils in reading their exercises and listening to instruction and criticism from the teacher. For Monday's lesson the pupils are asked to **Monday.** write a story. Each pupil chooses his own subject. The following is a specimen:—

Once as I was walking through a field, I met a poor little girl. I asked her what her name was and she said her name was Katie Brown. Her clothes were ragged and torn, and her lips were blue with cold. I asked her if she had a mother. She said her mother and father were dead and she was left alone to seek her fortune. Would you like to come with me? Oh yes said the little girl will you take me to your house? Yes I shall be glad to take you with me. Where is your house said the little girl. My house is up on that hill. I brought the little girl up to my house and let her warm herself I gave her something to eat. I put a dress of mine on to her and told her she could keep it. She lived with me and went to school every day. After that she was a good scholar. And we played every day together.

When such exercises as these reach the teacher's desk, she will see that no use has been made of quotation marks, and that the punctuation must be changed to correspond. But every day her pupils have been reading stories full of conversations marked and punctuated properly. Their attention has not been called to such points, and thousands of pupils finish the second and third readers every year, and have been "drilled" on the pieces until they know them by heart, who were never told that such a thing as a quotation mark existed. When, however, the use of such forms of punctuation is understood, pupils will write conversations as readily as plain narrative. For instance, the teacher may ask John to tell something about the schoolroom. John says, The schoolroom has four windows. The teacher asks the class to write the statement, the room has four windows, and then the double statement, John says. "The room has four windows,"

LANGUAGE. 51

telling them to look in their readers for such forms and punctuation. In the pupil's exercise just given, the quotation is divided, — "Oh, yes," being separated from the rest by *said the little girl.* To write it correctly requires a knowledge of capitalization and punctuation beyond that required for John's statement concerning the windows. Consequently, the work of correction will be taken up in this exercise by bringing about such a change as is indicated by this form: "Would you like to come with me?" "Oh, yes!" said the little girl, "Will you take me to your house?" "Yes, I shall be glad to take you with me." "Where is your house?" said the little girl. "My house is up on that hill." To accomplish this, more than one Monday will be necessary, but the pupils of Grade III. are capable of it.

The teacher for Tuesday's exercise exhibits a picture, or draws one upon the board. Each pupil writes detached sentences describing it, as follow: —

Tuesday.

Two boys are in a boat. The boat is on a pond. There is a dog in the boat. One of the boys has lost his hat in the water. The other boy has taken off his coat. The dog jumps into the water and gets the hat. The water is not very deep; one boy dips his hand into the water. I think the water feels cool. I hope he will not fall in.

The mechanical part of this original composition has been learned in Grade II. Still, if found necessary to dwell upon periods and capitalization, the exercise can be varied with dictation work, in which the attention is entirely given to the mechanical portion and to spelling. For the latter purpose let John rise, read the first and succeeding sentences, spelling each word, mentioning capitals and punctuation. Change slates and correct. For a written exercise, let the class copy that description of the picture which exhibits the best sentences properly executed. Later in the year the class will connect the detached sentences given above, or others like them, making a narrative, which will include all the objects shown in the pictures. A teacher who can draw will easily make a picture off-hand, which the class will be eager to describe in answer to questions which she may ask. Encourage the children to bring to school pictures or advertisement cards, and make each exhibition a language-exercise.

A short story is read aloud, on Wednesday, by the teacher once. Then the pupils write as much of it on their slates as they remember. They write busily ten or fifteen minutes. Then all stop writing, and listen while several of the stories are read aloud. In reading aloud nothing is suggested as to proper mechanical execution. When the class comes up from Grade II., try such an exercise, and on looking at a few slates you will quickly see what they know about punctuation and capitalization, and what they must still be taught. The following exercise from a story read by the teacher shows the writer's knowledge and ignorance : —

Wednesday.

LANGUAGE.

A fox after running till he was out of breath, begged a man to show him a place to hide. He showed him his hut and let him hide under his bed. He told the fox he would not tell. Soon after the hunters came along and asked him if he had seen the fox. He shook his head and pointed. The fox had just time enough to escape out of a window that was on the other side of the hut. A few days after the man met the fox and said, why did you leave my hut for without thanking me for saving your life. You did not tell the truth said the fox. I did not tell where you were. No said the fox but you pointed that is all that deaf and dumb people do when they tell lies.

Thursday is correction day, when the important features of the week's work are commented upon. Keep the poorest papers and copy them upon the board. Let the pupils correct them aloud. That corrections may be free, do not write the names of the authors of the exercises. Fullness of spontaneous correction tests the knowledge of the class. Note failure to correct certain mistakes, and bring in the same points the next week. Corrected sentences can be written on the pupils' slates. Take this day for common and vulgar errors, correcting what has been improperly spoken in the class-room, or what passes outside for correct speech. Street signs furnish an amusing commentary on popular knowledge or ignorance, especially the use of the apostrophe as a sign of the plural, where no thought of possession is intended. Pupils make very good critics when their attention is turned in the proper direction; but many a teacher who "drills" her class on the names of all the

Thursday.

coral reefs of the South Pacific never thinks of the familiar misnomers of the village street, or the journalistic freaks of the special reporter. This is also an appropriate time to test the knowledge of the class in writing sentences from oral dictation. Dictate sentences, making no mention of capitalization or punctuation, calling upon the class to supply them. Teach here the signs of the possessive case, both in the singular and in the plural of regularly formed words, and the punctuation marks not already familiar. Avoid, however, definitions of the possessive in a technical form. See that such sentences are written properly: "John gave William and I Franks shoes, the childrens books," etc. Continue the correction of school vulgarisms, and interest your class in the use of correct forms of speech by making error ridiculous.

Friday is letter day. When the letters are written let them be directed. It may not be practicable to sup-

Friday. ply envelopes for each week's exercises; but the address can be written on the back of the folded letter. Change the style of address from time to time. Practice in this grade the different forms of address inside the sheet, according to the degree of acquaintance and corresponding formality. A teacher once said: "Write a letter to your mother to-day; make believe she is away from home, and tell her what has happened in her absence." The following was one response:—

CLINTON, MASS., May 22, 1885.

DEAR MOTHER, — I am going to tell you what happened at home. Last night all the clothes fell down on the ground and they got dirty. When I went to bed I heard a great noise in the kitchen. When I got up it was the cat. The cat broke the sugar-bowl and a cup, and she broke the lamp too. I planted some seeds when you went away and they are very nice, they are coming up. Mother I would like you to come home Saturday afternoon. I want you to visit my school Wednesday afternoon. It is public day. I am going to speak a piece.
    Good bye,
      Your daughter,   L. C.

To vary the week's programme a lesson like any of the following is sometimes given. The teacher writes upon the blackboard a short story or part of a long one. The sentences are written incorrectly, capitals are misplaced, punctuation marks omitted, words misspelled, etc: "A man caught a little fish let me Go sed the fish til i am larger. i shall soon be a large fish Then you can catch Me agen but the man sed, You wil then no to much too bite." Sometimes a story is written on the board in the following manner, and the pupils copy it on their slates, supplying the words omitted: "Tom and — lived — the water. They — not swim so — mother — them — must — go alone — the —. Tom — a good — and — as — was —; but — went — the —. He — in — and was —. His mother was — that — did — mind," etc.

Occasionally divide the school into six or eight divisions; give each division a different word, as palace, princess, queen, etc. Then let the children when called upon in each division rise and give a sentence containing the word assigned to their division.

In addition to purely literary work in Grade III., continue object-teaching by means of pictures. Allow sentences spoken to be written on slates or preserved on paper. Thus on the Lion the teacher will call out these facts, supposing that the children have seen a lion in a menagerie, or that the teacher has a picture of one.

The lion belongs to the cat family. He comes from Africa; some are found in Asia. They live in pairs. They are from six to eight feet long. They weigh from four to five hundred pounds. Their color is a tawny yellow. The male lion has a mane of long hair; the female has no mane. They have thirty teeth, sharp and pointed, like those of a cat, so that they can tear flesh with them. They have a rough tongue for the same purpose. The lion has great strength and can carry a calf or sheep in his mouth. The lion springs upon his prey like a cat. He can spring twenty feet at one bound. The lion has a terrible roar. At night he causes other animals to tremble by his roar. He can see well at night like a cat. He swings his long tail when he is angry like a cat. His tail is strong enough to strike a man down with one blow.

This will tell the class something about silk : —

Silk is the web of the silk-worm. The worm feeds on mulberry leaves. After eating eight weeks, the worm begins to spin. The thread is stronger than a spider's web. The worm spins the thread around itself in the form of a case. This is called the cocoon. The cocoon is about an inch long. The worm is an insect like the caterpillar. It changes two or three times, and at last makes a hole in the cocoon and flies out, lays eggs, and dies. To prevent the worm from making a hole in it the cocoon is placed in a heated oven; the insect is then killed. The threads of the cocoons are loosened in hot water, and then wound upon a reel. They are then sorted and are ready for spinning. The web of a single cocoon is from three to five hundred yards long. Silk is raised in Asia, Europe, and in the United States, and is manufactured in France and in this country. It is used to make ribbons, handkerchiefs, gloves, stockings, shawls, dresses, sewing-silk, and many other articles.

Begin geographical instruction in this grade. Apply the points of the compass to the schoolroom, and names to local geographical objects, il- **Geogra-** lustrating without much definition the earth's **phy.** shape, sunrise, sunset, horizon, zenith, etc. Illustrate ideas of boundary and distance by the adjacent towns, even by objects within sight, the maps or pictures upon the walls, etc. Let pupils associate names of county, state, country, with their own town or city, and begin here descriptions of local industries. Make this a language-exercise in all cases, and see that facts are stated in the form of full and grammatical sentences. As " busy work " let pupils draw and cut out triangles, squares, circles, and polygons. Show their differences, but avoid technical definitions. Continue oral instruction in physiology, connecting it with hygiene (where no text-book is supplied), and take whatever opportunity offers to inculcate good school morals, especially kindness and courtesy to schoolmates, as well as the more obvious requirements of cleanliness, veracity, and purity of word and act.

It is important that the memory be trained in connection with language-exercise. For this pur-
Declamation. pose the teacher of Grade III. will give out verses or other short selections to be committed to memory and spoken at proper intervals. Begin with a single verse of poetry, because that form of composition is more attractive to the young than prose. Avoid long selections: rather one verse a day than a long poem once a week. Select the best authors. In Germany the children learn at school the ballads and lyrics of such a poet as Schiller, and never forget them. See that the sentiment is as pure as the verse, and that lessons of patriotism, charity, courtesy, generosity, kindness, truthfulness, humanity, are learned from those who tell us: —

> "Never to blend our pleasure or our pride
> With sorrow of the meanest thing that feels."

Grades IV. and V. — Fourth and Fifth Years.

As there is no particular distinction in the work of these grades, they are united for our present purpose. The general course of instruction changes here; books are substituted for oral instruction, and primary work ceases. Still, in language-exercise the teacher is not released from playing the leading *rôle*. Her work in this department must continue to be largely oral, and, that it may be successful, she must extend the domain of her own activity. It is true that the dictionary takes the place of the teacher's definition. At the beginning of the year she should prepare her class for the intelligent use of the dictionary, calling attention to the divisions of words, marks of accent, signs or synonyms of pronunciation, and whatever may be technical in the particular book used. Each pupil should be provided with one, or the unabridged copy on the teacher's desk should be open to unrestricted consultation by the class.

Your pupils have been prepared in the lower grades for the more serious tasks now before them. See that they are not lacking in practical acquaintance with the comma, period, question and surprise marks, hyphen, apostrophe in its various uses, quotation marks, and the common abbreviations. They can write a letter, can describe with a certain degree of fullness objects or pictures, can take down with reasonable accuracy what is read to them of simple style and diction. They know something of geography, physiology, color, form, measure, relative size and distance. They have obtained information concerning the more common animals, have described their uses and habits, and have seen how food, clothing, pleasure, and labor are procured from them. As their study of the geographical text-book continues, they read of vegetables, minerals, animals, and manufactures, which are mentioned but not described, belonging to countries briefly noticed, and exported from cities whose names are all the pupils know of them. This vast hiatus between what is told and what is untold is our teacher's opportunity. To merely mention it indicates a programme. This consists in filling out the bare outline of the text, by telling what the things *are* whose existence only is mentioned. Thus the lumber product of Maine, the granite quarries of New Hampshire and Massachusetts, the maple-sugar and marble product of Vermont, the fisheries of Massachusetts, the manufactures of cotton, ship-building, the cure and manufacture of leather, are only alluded to in books, and the desire to know is stimulated but not satisfied by the statement that Lowell is called the Manchester of America, or that Nantucket was a famous whaling port.

The teacher has in a primary geography a ready guide to language exercise. She is not limited to it, however. She should at all events have a logical plan of her own, and adhere to it. Teachers of intermediate grades, who have text-books thrust into their hands, are in danger of confining their work to them, or of throwing it on to the class. So far as language-work, however, is concerned, she is almost entirely put upon her own resources. The success or failure of her attempts at oral language-exercise will depend upon herself. "There is, perhaps, no practice better adapted to insure effective oral teaching," says one author, "than diligent preparation of the lessons which the teacher intends to give her pupils;" and again: "Experience daily proves that an unprepared lesson, or what may be termed extempore teaching, is sure to be vague, diffuse, and shallow; and on the other hand that a well-prepared lesson is generally clear, to the point, and given with spirit and effect." In arranging a plan of instruction the *method* is not new. It should still be oral and objective; it is only the scope which is extended, until the library is drawn upon in the course of the teacher's and pupil's combined interest in investigation.

From his entrance to school, the attention of the child has been directed to objects, at first within the schoolroom, and then beyond its walls as his power of observation increases. *Apply the principles of attention to language-exercise of the fourth grade.* The universe is one vast object-lesson, and yet teachers ask plaintively, "What shall we teach in language? Where shall we look for subject-matter?" Let the teacher first ask herself in what direction her own tastes lead her. What she enjoys she will teach well; what she does not like she will teach, if she must, perfunctorily, and therefore unsuccessfully. The secret of reasonable supervision lies in giving full play to the natural bent and predominating tastes of teachers, where they have any; where they have none, and are incapable of inspiration, the case with them is indeed hopeless. As means of development, object-teaching has borne its share in the work of the previous grades. We now consider it as a source of information, the communication of which serves to produce correct speech in both its oral and written forms.

When your class come into the fourth grade, discover by experiment what they can do. Illustrate by example their knowledge of punctuation, of the principles of letter-writing, of the correct use of every-day forms of speech, of abbreviations and capitals. Do not be surprised if they make occasional and even frequent blunders; neither are their elders exempt from error. After the first month of such trial, begin your own course of language-work. Provide each of your pupils with a blank book. Tell them that only the best exercises of the class on any subject will be written therein. Begin with what is common and near at hand. In addition to the animals, plants, vegetables, minerals, which you will take up in the course of your instruction in geography, add to your repertory such familiar objects as the following: *pen, candle, match, honey, sealing-wax, pin, ink, paper, milk, coral, ivory, whalebone, camphor, cork, acorn, needle, bell.* Show a lead-pencil and ask of what it is composed. Tell where the lead is found, what other name may be given to it, how it appears when dug from the earth, where the wood of the pencil comes from, of what shape are the trees, what early mention is made of them, how the wood is prepared for use, what different operations are required to prepare the wood for the lead; split a pencil and show the strips and the groove. Have the statements made in clear, compact sentences written on slates, to be transferred to the blank book. A drop of water will lead to remarks, drawn from pupils if possible, upon its springs and sources, the various kinds and conditions in which it is found, its qualities and uses, the names of the larger bodies, and of such as may be within the personal knowledge of the class. Draw out answers from pupils before giving them information. When those answers are correct let them be written down. When many such statements are made on any one subject, combine those statements into a description, and let that be a weekly exercise, the result to be written in the book. Stimulate the pupil's interest by making him seem to inform you of what you perhaps do not know. Never repress any attempt to talk, however rude or uncouth it may be. Correct, but do not ridicule.

Choose the subjects for these daily talks and exercises according to your own taste and familiarity with them. Proceed in all cases from the simple to the more complicated, and begin at home before going abroad. If you take animals, divide them into branches, classes, orders, and families; mark the differences, as you proceed, of mammals, birds, reptiles, and fishes; show the features certain families have in common; illustrate traits of character by anecdotes, and before offering information of your own, draw it from the pupil by questions. Show pictures when possible, and make the language-exercise an object-lesson first, a writing-exercise later. Flowers, vegetables, minerals, will take their turn in your programme, and be submitted to similar treatment. Suit the description of qualities to the age and development of your pupils; use the words *opaque, porous, soluble, nutritious, brittle, transparent, elastic, odorous*. Whenever you can, explain those words so that your pupils can apply them correctly the next time they appropriately occur. You will find the following words applicable to a piece of refined sugar: white, sweet, sparkling, crystalline, solid, fusible, soluble, shapeless, hard, refined, nutritious, crumbling, opaque, vegetable (substance), brittle. There is among them hardly a word that may not be made plain to your pupils by a few words of explanation, nor one that they will not be eager and able to use in describing some other vegetable or mineral substance.

Take an interest in what you are teaching, and your class will feel the contagion. You can inspire them to original investigation, and your pupils of Grade V. will acquire a fund of information which grammar scholars of higher grades once failed to possess. The year represented by Grade IV. will best be occupied with simple exercises, in which the pupil's slender fund of knowledge is supplemented by the teacher's larger hoard. As he reaches the fifth grade, inspire him to find out for himself what lies within reach of every schoolboy. Let him bring to school the fruit of his investigation, and the best essay will merit preservation in the blank book ; or, when a subject has been studied, let the teacher ask questions, and the simple answers of the class may be written down as given, or made over into a narrative form. Here are certain questions and answers about the Camel, which may serve as a guide for class work. It is too much to expect a teacher to make a dialogue concerning the objects of an entire year's study; but suppose that your class have read about the camel, and that each one has acquired some fact which he gives in answer to the teacher's question ; or the teacher may bring an encyclopædia into school, and, having read to the class about the camel, call for facts in the pupil's own language: —

1. Of what is the camel a native?
Ans. Of the desert countries of southwestern Asia, whence it spread over the arid regions of the eastern hemisphere. (What do you mean by "arid"?)

2. What is it sometimes called?
Ans. "The Ship of the Desert."

3. Why is it so called?
Ans. Because it carries heavy loads over the desert, where nothing could take its place. (Some precocious child answers: "Where it is the only means of locomotion.")

4. How is it prepared for its life in the desert?
First Answer. Its teeth are wonderfully suited for tearing apart and masticating the coarse, dry shrubs on which it feeds.
(*Question:* What do mean by masticating?)

Second Answer. Its nostrils can be opened or shut at will, and thus the organ of smell, which is very acute, is defended against the hot sand which sweeps over the desert.

Third Answer. The toes, except the two forming the foot, are connected by a broad, elastic pad, which buoys the camel up as it moves over the yielding surface of the desert.

Fourth Answer. The hump or humps on the camel's back are masses of fat, forming a reserve of nourishment to be used when other supplies fail. (In reply to this statement, which is denied by some authorities, the teacher will tell her class that in a recent war in Afghanistan sixty thousand camels died of starvation and thirst.)

Fifth Answer. The stomach contains cells in which water can be stored.

5. Describe the camel.

Ans. JOHN. The camel is about eight feet high.

MARY. It is of a dark brown or yellowish color.

JAMES. It has teeth like a dog.

FRANK. The camel chews the cud like the cow.

SARAH. It has cushions on its knees, so that it can kneel down to receive its load.

Question. How is the camel taught to kneel?

Ans. The young camel's legs are bent under it every day by its owner, until it kneels when commanded. They are also taught to fast for five or six days at a time, to prepare them for their life on the desert.

6. How heavy a weight can the camel carry?

CHARLES. From five hundred to one thousand pounds.

EDWARD. They are expected to carry their load twenty-five miles a day for three days, without water.

JENNIE. Some camels can travel fifty miles a day for five days without drinking.

PETER. When too heavily laden the camel refuses to rise from its knees, but when on the march it is **exceedingly patient,** only yielding beneath its load to die.

7. How does the camel meet a storm?

Ans. When overtaken by the simoon, or sand-storm, it falls upon its knees, and, stretching its neck along the sand, closes its nostrils and remains thus motionless until the air is clear.

8. How is the driver protected at this time?

Ans. The driver crouches behind the camel, wrapped in his mantle.

9. How does the dromedary differ from the camel?

Ans. It is found in Arabia, and has but one hump. It is much more fleet than the camel, and has finer hair and a more elegant form. It can carry its driver, when necessary, one hundred miles a day. The dromedary is to the camel as a race-horse to a cart-horse.

10. How do we know that the camel was one of the earliest animals subdued by man for his use?

Ans. Because it is mentioned in the oldest records of the human race, six thousand camels forming part of the wealth of Job. The trace of no wild camel has been found, from which the tame species could have been derived, as is the case with all other domestic animals.

11. Is the camel an amiable creature?

Ans. No, it is very vicious and bad-tempered. They often fight with each other. They are so obstinate that they often sink on their knees, and no amount of beating will get them up until they choose to rise.

12. What do they live upon?

Ans. Date leaves, and a kind of cake made of the dates; beans, and prickly shrubs.

13. What can you say of its milk?

Ans. It is a favorite drink, and is often made into butter. Its flesh is cut up and salted for food.

14. What is manufactured from the camel?

Ans. The hair is made into small brushes used by painters. The hide is made into very strong leather. The Arabs shear their camels every summer, and weave the hair into tent-coverings and clothing.

SUSAN. My mother has a camel's-hair shawl.

15. How can you show that the camel is a native of the desert?

Ans. Because all camels dislike to cross a stream of water or marshy ground, so that their owners deceive them by spreading tent-cloths upon damp ground which they wish them to pass over.

16. What is the motion of a camel?

Ans. The camel moves first the legs on the right side, then the two on the left side, giving its body a swaying motion, which causes in people unaccustomed to the motion a feeling like seasickness.

Here follow some questions upon the Elephant:—

1. What do we notice particularly in the elephant?

Ans. The size of the body, the teeth, and the proboscis or trunk.

2. What is the trunk?

Ans. It is a huge extension of the nose and upper lip, from six to eight feet long, formed of a mass of muscles. These muscles number nearly forty thousand. They are so arranged as to produce the greatest possible diversity of motion.

3. What does the end of the trunk contain?

Ans. The end of the trunk contains the two openings of the nostrils by which the elephant breathes when swimming. It fills its trunk with water through these nostrils, and then throws the water into its mouth or over its body.

4. How does the trunk end?

Ans. In something like a finger, of great delicacy of touch.

5. To what may you compare it?

Ans. It forms an organ in many respects like the human hand. The elephant smells with it also.

6. How does the elephant use this finger?

Ans. With it the elephant collects food, discovers snares, and strikes down its enemy. It can also pick up a pin or open a door with its proboscis.

7. From what is the word "trunk" derived?

Ans. From a French word meaning *trumpet*, because the elephant utters through this organ a shrill, trumpet-like sound when enraged.

8. How much does the elephant depend upon its trunk?

Ans. Without it the elephant could not feed itself. It is therefore very cautious in its use.

9. How many teeth has the elephant?

Ans. Two incisors, or tusks, and six molars. As the latter are gradually worn away others appear, and the elephant may be said to be always teething.

10. Of what are the tusks composed?

Ans. Of ivory. They grow during the animal's life, and sometimes weigh two hundred pounds. They are hollow for a part of their length.

11. Of what use are they?

Ans. The elephant uses them in fighting, and has thrown a tiger thirty feet into the air with them. They are useful in tearing down trees, upon the leaves of which the elephant feeds. In Ceylon, where the elephant lives on grass, it has no tusks.

12. Has the elephant a large brain?

Ans. It is rather small; but the bones of the skull are very large, in order to support the powerful muscles of the head and trunk.

13. How much does the elephant weigh at full size?

Ans. Fully three tons, and stands eleven feet in height.

14. How long does the elephant live?

Ans. It grows for thirty years, and lives more than one hundred. Some have lived one hundred and thirty years in captivity.

15. How does the African differ from the Asiatic elephant?

Ans. The ears of the former are very large, completely covering the shoulders when thrown back. They have been known to be three and one half feet in length by two and one half feet wide. The African stands higher, and his tusks are heavier.

16. How much ivory is imported?

Ans. England imports 1,200,000 lbs. yearly, to obtain which 30,000 animals are killed. Perhaps 100,000 a year supply the entire world.

17. For what has the elephant been used?

Ans. By the ancient nations, like the Romans, in war. By the natives of Asia, to drive off invaders. Since fire-arms came into use, elephants are employed to drag heavy cannon and carry baggage. They are also used in India to hunt tigers, the hunters sitting on the elephant's back in an open box, the driver being on the animal's back.

18. How are elephants caught?

Ans. They are driven into a large enclosure or *corral.* The entrance is then walled up, and the elephants rush wildly about, seeking means of escape. After a while they become tired, and tame elephants are let in, bearing a keeper. As the wild elephants mingle freely with the tame ones, they are thrown off their guard, and a rope, one end of which is attached to the neck of a tame elephant, is passed over each leg of the wild animal. It is then securely tied to the trunk of a tree. After a training of two months, in which the tame elephant assists, the captive may be ridden by the owner, and worked in four months.

19. Why are white elephants so valued?

Ans. Because they are so rare. In Siam the chief white elephant ranks next the queen, and before the heir apparent to the crown. (Tell your class that in the sixteenth century a war was waged in lower India, in which five kings were slain for the possession of a particular white elephant. Read accounts of their habits of bathing in herds, and the exploits of hunters like Cumming.)

Letter-Writing. The pupils of Grades IV. and V. will continue the practice of letter-writing. They are now prepared to pay some attention to style. Hence teach the division of the body of the letter into paragraphs. Show that a change in the thought or subject matter of the letters should be indicated by taking a new line; mark in some illustration upon the board the place of the first word in the new paragraph. Teach the abbreviations belonging to certain titles or offices. Let the children write imaginary letters, not like Toots to himself, but to personages enjoying titles of office, dignity, rank, etc. Make the style of address conform to the age, character, or office of the person addressed. Let the class answer advertisements found in newspapers for clerks, teachers, mechanics, artisans, agents, and state in modest terms the qualifications possessed by the applicant. Remove from all language-exercises anything cramped and formal, all the etiquette attending the " composition " of higher grades. Let the exercises be fresh while instructive, interesting while beneficial; invest them with the charm which you endeavor to throw around your work in all branches of study, and, while your pupils will know nothing of technical grammar, they will write a letter or read an essay which will show them to be, like the Emperor Sigismund, "above grammar."

On the following pages will be found a list of books of authority on themes suitable for language-exercises, together with the catalogue of a Teachers' Consulting Library.

BOOKS OF AUTHORITY ON TOPICS SUITABLE FOR LANGUAGE-EXERCISE.

All Encyclopædias.
Manual of Object Teaching:	*Calkins.*
Primary Object Lessons:	"
Lessons on Objects:	*Sheldon.*
Elementary Instruction:	"
Development Lessons:	*DeGraff.*
Object Lessons:	*Walker; Welch.*
Cambridge Information Cards.	*Lee & Shepard.*
Fairy Land of Science:	*Buckley.*
Matter and Force:	*Tyndall.*
Geological Story:	*Dana.*
Science Primers.	*Appletons.*
Oral Lessons in Science:	*Barnard.*
Familiar Science;	*Brewer.*
Child's Book of Nature:	*Hooker.*
Child's Book of Natural History:	*Carll.*
Natural History:	*Harpers.*
Animal Physiology:	*Angell; Cleland.*
Talks with my Boys:	*Mowry.*

Natural History Series and Manual: *Prang*.
Natural History Reader: *Johonnot*.
Glimpses of the Animated World: "
How Plants Behave: *Gray*.
How Plants Grow: "
Manuals for Teachers: *Eldredge & Bro*.
Methods of Teaching: *Swett*.
Object Lessons on Human Body: *Lovell & Co*.
Picture and Word Cards: *Davis*.
Word Method in Number: *Sanford*.
Seven Little Sisters: *Andrews*.
Geographical Readers: *Philip*.
Voices for the Speechless (for memorizing).
Memory Gems: *Lambert*.
Little Gems: *Potter & Ainsworth*.
Selections for Little Folks: *Eldredge & Co*.
Ballads and Lyrics: *Lodge*.

TEACHERS' CONSULTING LIBRARY.

Education as a Science :	*Bain.*
Art of School Management :	*Baldwin.*
Calderwood on Teaching.	
Early and Infant Education :	*Currie.*
School Room Guide :	*DeGraff.*
Lectures on Teaching :	*Fitch.*
Morals and Manners :	*Gow.*
In the School Room :	*Hart.*
Errors in the Use of English :	*Hodgson.*
School Management :	*Kellogg.*
Comenius ; His Life, etc. :	*Laurie.*
Talks with Teachers :	*Mayo.*
Teacher and Parent :	*Northend.*
Science of Education :	*Ogden.*
Teacher's Manual :	*Orcutt.*
Quincy Methods Illustrated :	*Patridge.*
Science and Art of Education :	*J. Payne.*
Lectures on Education :	"
School Supervision :	*W. H. Payne.*

After Kindergarden, What?   *Peabody and Mann.*
Talks with Teachers :   *Parker.*
Educational Reformers :   *Quick.*
Outlines of Psychology :   *Sully.*
Philosphy of Education :   *Tate.*
Methods of Instruction :   *Wickersham.*
Lectures on Pedagogy :   *Hailman.*
Methods of History :   *Hall.*
Education :   *Spencer.*
Principles and Practice of Teaching : *Johonnot.*
Vocal and Physical Training :   *Munroe.*
Sound Bodies for Boys and Girls :   *Blaikie.*
Theory and Practice of Teaching :   *Thring.*
Lessons on Manners :   *Wiggin.*
School Management :   *Landon.*
Education by Doing :   *Johnson.*
School Hygiene, Lectures on.
Education and Manual Industry :   *MacArthur.*

Lee and Shepard's Popular Handbooks.

Price, each, in cloth, 50 cents, except when other price is given.

Forgotten Meanings; or, An Hour with a Dictionary. By ALFRED WAITES, author of "Historical Student's Manual."

Handbook of Elocution Simplified. By WALTER K. FOBES, with an Introduction by GEORGE M. BAKER.

Handbook of English Synonyms. With an Appendix, showing the Correct Use of Prepositions; also a Collection of Foreign Phrases. By LOOMIS J. CAMPBELL.

Handbook of Conversation. Its Faults and its Graces. Compiled by ANDREW P. PEABODY, D.D., LL.D. Comprising: (1) Dr. PEABODY'S Address; (2) Mr. TRENCH'S Lecture; (3) Mr. PARRY GWYNNE'S "A Word to the Wise; or, Hints on the Current Improprieties of Expression in Reading and Writing;" (4) Mistakes and Improprieties of Speaking and Writing Corrected.

Handbook of Punctuation and other Typographical Matters. For the Use of Printers, Authors, Teachers, and Scholars. By MARSHALL T. BIGELOW, corrector at the University Press, Cambridge, Mass.

Handbook of Blunders. Designed to prevent 1,000 common blunders in writing and speaking. By HARLAN H. BALLARD, A.M., principal of Lenox Academy, Lenox, Mass.

Broken English. A Frenchman's Struggle in the English Language. Instructive as a handbook of French conversation. By Professor E. C. DUBOIS.

Beginnings with the Microscope. A working handbook containing simple instructions in the art and method of using the microscope, and preparing articles for examination. By WALTER P. MANTON.

Field Botany. A Handbook for the Collector. Containing instructions for gathering and preserving Plants, and the formation of an Herbarium. Also complete instructions in Leaf Photography, Plant Printing, and the Skeletonizing of Leaves. By WALTER P. MANTON.

Taxidermy without a Teacher. Comprising a complete manual of instructions for Preparing and Preserving Birds, Animals, and Fishes, with a chapter on Hunting and Hygiene; together with instructions for Preserving Eggs, and Making Skeletons, and a number of valuable recipes. By WALTER P. MANTON.

Insects. How to Catch and how to Prepare them for the Cabinet. A Manual of Instruction for the Field-Naturalist. By W. P. MANTON.

What is to be Done? A Handbook for the Nursery, with Useful Hints for Children and Adults. By ROBERT B. DIXON, M.D.

Handbook of Wood Engraving. With practical instructions in the art, for persons wishing to learn without an instructor. By WILLIAM A. EMERSON. Illustrated. Price $1.00.

Five-Minute Recitations. Prepared by WALTER K. FOBES.

Five-Minute Declamations. Prepared by WALTER K. FOBES.

Warrington's Manual. Handbook of Legislative Practice for the Guidance of Public Meetings, etc. By WM. S. ROBINSON ("Warrington").

Sold by all booksellers and newsdealers, and sent by mail, postpaid, on receipt of price.

LEE AND SHEPARD, Publishers, Boston.

Lee and Shepard's Popular Handbooks.

Price, each, in cloth, 50 cents, except when other price is given.

Exercises for the Improvement of the Senses. For young children. By HORACE GRANT, author of "Arithmetic for Young Children." Edited by WILLARD SMALL.

Hints on Language in Connection with Sight-Reading and Writing in Primary and Intermediate Schools. By S. ARTHUR BENT, A.M., Superintendent of Public Schools, Clinton, Mass.

The Hunter's Handbook. Containing lists of provisions and camp paraphernalia, and hints on the fire, cooking-utensils, etc., with approved receipts for camp cookery. By "AN OLD HUNTER."

Universal Phonography; or, Shorthand by the "Allen Method." A self-instructor. By G. G. ALLEN.

Hints and Helps for those who Write, Print, or Read. By B. DREW, proof-reader.

Pronouncing Handbook of Three Thousand Words often Mispronounced. By R. SOULE and L. J. CAMPBELL.

Short Studies of American Authors. By THOMAS WENTWORTH HIGGINSON.

The Stars and the Earth; or, Thoughts upon Space, Time, and Eternity. With an introduction by THOMAS HILL, D.D., LL.D.

Handbook of the Earth. Natural Methods in Geography. By LOUISA PARSONS HOPKINS, teacher of normal methods in the Swain Free School, New Bedford.

Natural-History Plays. Dialogues and Recitations for School Exhibitions. By LOUISA P. HOPKINS.

The Telephone. An account of the phenomena of Electricity, Magnetism, and Sound, with directions for making a speaking-telephone. By Professor A. E. DOLBEAR.

Lessons on Manners. By EDITH E. WIGGIN.

Water Analysis. A Handbook for Water-Drinkers. By G. L. AUSTIN, M.D.

Handbook of Light Gymnastics. By LUCY B. HUNT, instructor in gymnastics at Smith (female) College, Northampton, Mass.

The Parlor Gardener. A Treatise on the House-Culture of Ornamental Plants. By CORNELIA J. RANDOLPH. With illustrations.

Whirlwinds, Cyclones, and Tornadoes. By WILLIAM MORRIS DAVIS, instructor in Harvard College. Illustrated.

Practical Boat-Sailing. By DOUGLAS FRAZAR. Classic size, $1.00. With numerous diagrams and illustrations.

Sold by all booksellers and newsdealers, and sent by mail, postpaid, on receipt of price.

LEE AND SHEPARD, Publishers, Boston.

www.ingramcontent.com/pod-product-compliance
Lightning Source LLC
Chambersburg PA
CBHW020335090426
42735CB00009B/1541